Beyond the Margins:

An Indispensable Guide for First-Time Freelance Writers, Designers, and Other Work-from-Home Professionals

Michael Kwan
michaelkwan.com

Formatted by Polgarus Studio

Table of Contents

Introduction

When I first embarked on this journey as a freelance writer, I didn't have anyone telling me what to expect, what to avoid or what to do in order to turn it into a viable full-time business. What resulted was an extended period of trial and error as I attempted to find my way through the murky waters of freelancing. While I had some experience with *writing* already, the freelance path represented largely uncharted territory and I surely made a few mistakes along the way.

You don't need to make the same mistakes.

If you are reading this book right now, then chances are you are interested in a career in freelancing. You may have been laid off from your regular job or there's something about your entrepreneurial spirit that has been left untapped. Whatever your motivation, you are seriously considering a career where you work from home, manage your own client list and pay yourself first and foremost. You've come to the right place.

Before we get started, perhaps I should introduce myself. My name is Michael Kwan. I have been producing content on the Internet since 1999, but I didn't parlay that writing experience into my own home-based business until early 2006. Since that time, my writing has been featured both online and offline in several different publications. These include Mobile Magazine, John Chow dot Com, Smartlife Blog, Green Home Therapy and Blogging Tips, among many others. You may have also read *Make Money Online: Roadmap of a Dot Com Mogul*, a book I co-authored with John Chow. I also run my own personal blog, *Beyond the Rhetoric*, which can be found at http://btr.michaelkwan.com. There, I write about food, freelancing, travel and a variety of other subjects.

And therein lies a critical distinction.

Someone who plays poker with friends on the weekends is not the same as a professional like Daniel Negreanu who plays poker for a living. Someone who plays golf recreationally is entirely different from a Tiger Woods or a Phil Mickelson. Similarly, there is a critical difference between the person who blogs for fun and the person who blogs professionally.

If you're reading this book, you probably want to be the latter.

There is a distinct learning curve when it comes to any professional endeavor and a freelance writing career is no exception. Had I known then what I know now, I probably would have pursued this career in a slightly different manner than I have. I still have room to grow, but I have learned a lot in these last few years about what it means to run a successful business out of my home.

Over the course of this book, I will be sharing several valuable tips in regards to building a freelance career. The focus and scope will be centered on freelance *writing*, since that's what I do, but the core guiding principles are easily applicable to other forms of freelancing as well: coding, designing, consulting and so on.

There is a world of opportunity out there; you just have to know how to capture it. Let's get down to work.

Chapter 1: Preparing to Enter the Freelance Arena

Before I can start offering any tips to people who are already freelancing, it is important to consider many of the major decisions that you'll make even before you take that initial leap of faith and pursue freelancing full-time. It's also very important to think about the major factors that will come into play very early in your career and these early decisions can be monumentally influential on how your freelance career will develop and evolve. Just as you may want to look at a map of the route before you head out on a road trip into unfamiliar territory, you'll want to take the Boy Scouts' approach to freelancing too: Always be prepared.

With that in mind, I have five critical tips that all prospective freelancers should keep in mind before they dip their proverbial toes in the water.

Decide If It's Right For You

Some people may assume that this step is largely unnecessary. After all, if you weren't interested in a career in freelance writing, you probably wouldn't be reading this book in the first place. However, far too many people dive head first into this kind of career without realizing that the career path doesn't really suit them. It's not a matter of ability but rather a matter of fit. Someone more inclined toward creative expression probably isn't going to be happy with a raw number-crunching position.

The single biggest tip I can give to anyone considering this line of work is to ask themselves whether it really is the kind of path they want to follow. The perceived freedoms and luxuries of working from home may certainly look attractive from the outside, but at the end of the day, you still want to enjoy the work that you do. This is still work, after all. So, here are some questions that you should ask yourself to help determine whether freelance writing, or any kind of home-based business for that matter, is the right kind of career path for you.

Are you prepared for unstable income month-to-month?

- When you work at a more conventional job, each paycheck is generally for about the same amount of money. In this way, you can expect to have an influx of X number of dollars every couple of weeks. Such is not the case with freelance writing. While there are certainly strategies you can employ to maintain a more stable positive cash flow—I'll discuss some later on in the book—there are going to months of feast and other months of famine. You need to be financially responsible enough to handle this natural ebb and flow of income.

Do you thrive on water cooler banter and co-worker camaraderie?

- There are networking events and social gatherings that you can attend, but the vast majority of the time spent as a freelance writer will be spent alone. You could rent some co-working space and social media platforms can help to keep you connected with the world, but freelance writing is largely a solo endeavor. Some people work better with the background hum of an office going through its paces. Some people perform better when they have co-workers on hand to double check the things that they are doing. If you are of this ilk, freelance writing may not be for you. On the flip side, if you tend to thrive when you can drive out the distractions, working solo may be a very good fit.

Can you motivate yourself to stay on task each and every day?

- Even if you don't have a supervisor breathing down your neck, the very nature of an office environment may be conducive to keeping you on task. When you're working out of a spare bedroom as your home office, there is no one peering over your shoulder. You need to be motivated enough to get yourself out of bed each morning, park yourself in front of your computer and actually get the job done. This sounds simple enough and it may be easy for the first week or two, but if freelance writing is going to be a career, you need to be motivated for years to come.

Will you be able to take on the different roles and responsibilities?

- If you've worked in a more typical office setting, then you'll know that there is a human resources department that does its thing, an accounting department that does its thing, a customer service department that does its thing and so on. When you venture out on a freelance writing career, guess what? You're all of those departments. You're also the administration department, the logistics department, the IT department, the secretary, the janitor, and everything in between. You will be wearing many different hats as a freelance writer that go well beyond the mere act of writing. These added responsibilities do help give you a sense of ownership of your work, but they can also be sources of tremendous stress. Are you prepared for this?

Can you continually produce quality content on a deadline?

- Some people choose to get into freelance writing, because writing is already a treasured hobby of theirs. That's fantastic. However, you also have to realize that writing for pleasure and writing as a career are two distinctly different beasts. When you write as a hobby, you write on your own time and there is no pressure to get it done *right this second.* That pressure can rear its ugly head during your professional career, though, and you'll need to be able to write quickly and efficiently time and time again if you want to be successful as a freelancer. The resulting articles not only have to be well-written; they have to be written on a deadline. Your clients can't wait around forever, right?

I don't mean to scare you away from a career in freelancing. It's one of the best decisions I've ever made in my life and I have no regrets about embarking on this wonderful journey. At the same time, I also realize that this kind of career happens to be a good fit for my personality, my preferences and my existing skill set. That may or may not be true with you. I couldn't possibly make it as a professional hockey player, because it's not in my nature. Before you dive into a freelance career, you need to determine above all else whether it is the right fit for you.

Treat It Like a Business, Not a Hobby

If you're embarking into the wonderful world of freelance writing as a means of supplementing your primary income, that's great. It means that you already have a consistent source of income from a more conventional job and any money that you earn writing for your clients is a bonus. If that's the case, this tip isn't really for you. However, if you would like freelance writing to be your full-time career, this tip is probably one of the more important ones for you to consider.

It sounds simple enough, but it's an idea that goes right over the head of many a beginning freelancer: treat this like a business and not like a hobby.

We all have our hobbies. Whether it's fixing our cars in the garage, playing video games in the den, or heading out to the park for a game of basketball, these are all leisurely activities that are to be taken leisurely. If you happen to miss a game of basketball with your friends, it's not the end of the world. If your tinkering with your hot rod costs you an extra half-second off the quarter mile time, you can always go back and fix it. These are hobbies and they are treated as such.

On the flip side, your freelance writing business is exactly that: a business. Don't discount its legitimacy or its value just because you happen to work out of your home and the company has a total employee count of one. Your business as a freelancer is no more or less legitimate than the grocery store around the corner or the corporate lawyer in his downtown office. If you don't believe in the legitimacy and importance of your business, you can't possibly expect your clients and colleagues to believe in it either.

So, what exactly does it mean to treat your freelancing career as a business? There are a few steps that you may want to take to aid not only in this mentality, but also in its operation.

First, you should register your business with your local government. This will vary from jurisdiction to jurisdiction and the laws governing this kind of thing are quite different in Canada versus the United States or other parts of the world. I am not a lawyer nor am I an accountant, so it's best that you seek professional advice and assistance should you feel so inclined. For Canadians, this could mean registering a business number, establishing a business name, and taking the necessary steps to start collecting sales tax. You'll need to ask yourself whether you'll be operating as a sole proprietorship or as a limited corporation. There are pros and cons to either approach, so you should weigh your options carefully.

Second, it may be prudent to design and order business cards. Again, this reiterates the fact that you are running a business and not merely pursuing a hobby. When you attend trade shows or networking events, it really helps when you have some professional business cards to exchange with the people that you meet. These contacts can result in great referrals for your business. How would you feel about dealing with a real estate agent or an interior designer if he or she did not have a business card?

Third, think about the expenses for your business as investments in their future. Yes, it helps that there are tax benefits to buying equipment and paying for services for your business, but don't go spending that money without a care in the world. Instead of thinking about them as personal expenditures, think about what sort of return on investment (ROI) you'll receive. Is it worthwhile to get a pro account with HootSuite? Should you pay for a premium membership with a local society? How important is it for you to buy a new computer, printer, or smartphone?

Other items that you may want to consider include setting up proper records for your income and expenses, establishing an online presence for your freelance writing brand, marketing your efforts accordingly to attract new customers, and so on. A hobby is just for fun, but a business comes down to the bottom line: are you making money?

If you simply sit in front of the computer for eight hours a day chatting on Facebook, you're not treating it like a business. You need to roll up your sleeves and get the job done.

Prepare a Proper Working Space

There's a misconception out there that freelance writers (and other work-from-home professionals) roll out of bed in their pajamas and slide over to a laptop at any room in the house. They might work from the living room while watching the big game or they might try to squeeze out one more article in the kitchen while preparing dinner. These are possibilities, to be sure, but they should not be the norm if you want to take your freelance career seriously. They're also not conducive to a healthy life-work balance.

For that reason alone, you should do your absolute best to prepare not only a proper working space, but a *dedicated* working space. This way, you can help to create both a mental and a physical separation between what you consider the world of work and what you would consider "home" life. Unlike a more conventional job where you can physically leave the work world at the office, a home office is exactly that: an office in the home. There needs to be a certain level of separation.

An ideal situation would be if you had a spare bedroom or den that you could convert into a dedicated home office. This way, you can have a physical door that separates your "home" from your "office." The other members of your household can then recognize that when the door is closed, you should not be disturbed. This helps you focus on your work when you need to do so. This isn't to say that you are totally inaccessible; it just means that you are no more or no less accessible than if you were at an office outside of your home. The other major advantage of having a separate room as your home office is that it can provide you with the additional space you may need for the different tasks you'll encounter. Filing cabinets, fax machines, and so on take space.

Depending on your living situation, this may not be possible. Even if you cannot have a spare bedroom as your home office, you should do your best to create some sort of boundary between what is considered your office and what is considered the rest of your home. Dedicate a corner of your bedroom to work. Have a desk in the family room with a folding room divider, if you can. This physical separation can prove invaluable not only to your productivity, but also to your comfort and your sanity. You will be spending several hours in this space, after all, so you should be comfortable.

On the subject of comfort, one of the best investments you can make is in a comfortable office chair. Ensure that it has proper cushioning and lumbar support. Adjustable arm rests, adjustable heights, and other options can prove very valuable. If you are not comfortable in your chair, you will not feel inclined to be as productive as possible. Following a similar line of thought, it helps to have a comfortable keyboard, mouse, and other accessories that are necessary for your day-to-day operations. Again, if these items are not comfortable under prolonged use, your mind can create a mental block preventing you from performing at your absolute best.

Early on in my freelance writing career, I worked anywhere I brought my laptop. I worked in the kitchen. I worked in the living room. I worked in my bedroom. I even worked from my bed. This may sound appealing, because of the flexibility and versatility, but it was ultimately a detriment to my productivity and my mental health. A proper working space away from the rest of the home helps to put your brain in "work mode," and that's precisely what you need if you want to be successful in your freelancing.

Recognize the Different Hats You'll Wear

Going back to the example of a freelance writer, your freelance career will consist of so much more than "just" writing. Sure, the writing aspect will occupy a great deal of your time, as you sit down at the computer and compose those wonderful articles, press releases, and website copy material. However, you'll find that your role as a small business owner is quite different than if you were, say, hired as a reporter for a local newspaper.

Instead of taking on just one set of responsibilities in the one role that you might occupy in a conventional job, you'll find that your freelance business is *a full-fledged business.* As such, you will quickly become responsible for all the different aspects of running that business. This may change as your business grows and evolves, as you may be able to generate enough income to start hiring employees and sub-contractors, but nearly all the roles will be occupied by you in the early stages. You'll be wearing many different "hats" each and every day.

So, what can you expect beyond the core task of writing (or your other chosen freelance profession)?

- **Customer Service**: As a freelancer, you'll likely be juggling more than one project at a time. You'll likely have more than one client at a time, and each of them will feel that he or she should be your priority.

Depending on how you choose to run your business, customer service may entail keeping up with the e-mail messages flooding your inbox. It may also include faxes, telephone calls, social media conversations, instant messages, and so many other avenues for communication. You must do what you can to keep your customers happy while also keeping your own bottom line (and sanity) in check.

- **Office Management**: Do you need some more pens and paper? Does the printer need more ink? Is it time to pay the Internet service provider again? It's highly unlikely that you'll be hiring an administrative assistant to handle many of these everyday concerns, at least in the early stages, so you must take on the role of office manager. This includes ordering new supplies when needed, keeping the home office neat and tidy, and ensuring that your logistical matters are handled appropriately.

- **Accounting**: Even if you are going to hire a professional accountant to "manage your books," you still have many accounting responsibilities. Your accountant can help you set up your books and prepare your income tax returns each year, but the maintenance of these books is your responsibility. This is true of both expenses and revenue, as well as all the other smaller tasks that occur in-between.

- **Technical Support**: When you are having trouble with your equipment in a conventional office, you can usually ask for help from "the IT guy." These specialists can help you understand why your computer is acting up, why it's not recognizing the new external hard drive, or any number of other technology issues. When you're on your own as a freelancer, the task of troubleshooting falls on your shoulders.

- **Marketing and Advertising**: How are you going to get the word out about your business? How are you going to attract new customers? While this role would normally fall on the marketing department, *you are the marketing department* for your freelance business. This includes not only the responsibility of coming up with an appropriate ad campaign (if that's what you want to do), but also its implementation and performance tracking.

- **Website Management**: If you want to be taken seriously as a freelancer, you'll want to set up your own website on your own domain. There are countless different frameworks and content management systems you can consider, but the task ultimately falls on you to create, oversee, and maintain that website. Some of these tasks can be outsourced, of course, but the initial and final responsibility represent another hat you'll be wearing. This also includes related tasks like domain registration, web hosting, search engine optimization, database management, and so forth. My friend Dave

Jacquart at ShiftUP Consulting (shiftup.ca) can help you with all that too. Just let him know I sent you.

And these are just a few examples of the different hats you'll be wearing. Depending on the specifics of your industry and your business, you may find yourself with many more hats. Are you prepared for this kind of responsibility?

Set Quantifiable Goals with Specific Timelines

If you were planning on opening a swanky new restaurant in the hottest part of town, you wouldn't go in there with the mindset of a limitless budget. You wouldn't invest all that time and money with an outlook of "we'll see how it goes." That doesn't make good business sense and no bank would approve your business loan if you approached them with that idea. The exact same philosophy should be applied to your freelancing business.

Many freelance writers, artists, designers, and coders enter the industry with a completely open mind and a completely open set of expectations. They don't write down exactly how they're going to go about running this business and how much they expect to make in their first year of operation. This is like going on a treasure hunt without a map or trying to navigate through the Tokyo subway system blindfolded.

Other freelancers start out with very vague goals. They may tell themselves that they want to make "a full-time income" with this business after they've worked on it "for a while." The trouble with these kinds of goals is that it can be very difficult to determine whether you've achieved them. It can also be very easy to come up with a series of excuses, because "for a while" can be interpreted a million different ways.

This is why it is so important to define what are known as "S.M.A.R.T." goals right from the get-go. S.M.A.R.T. goals are **Specific, Measurable, Attainable, Relevant,** and **Time-oriented.**

A **specific** goal focuses on one particular area rather than having a global focus. This is why you will likely have several goals that are constantly updated over the course of your career.

It's also important that your goal is **measurable,** so you can know exactly whether or not it has been achieved. Rather than say that you want to make "a full-time income," you can say that you want to earn "an annual net income of $50,000."

The goal needs to be **attainable** and realistic. It's unlikely you'll make a million dollars in your first year. You don't want to set your goals too lofty as they'd be utterly out of reach.

The goals need to be **relevant,** relating back specifically to your business and its long-term outlook. How does this smaller goal fit in with your longer term goals?

And finally, the goal needs to be **time-oriented.** It needs a deadline. Otherwise, it becomes a goal to be achieved "someday." And guess what? "Someday" never comes.

The quantifiable goals that you set for yourself fit in with an overall business plan. Remember that your freelance business is no different than a conventional brick-and-mortar operation. And it should be taken just as seriously. Freelancing is not a waypoint. It's a career and it's a business.

Chapter 2: Finding Work and Making Some Money

So, now you've made the educated decision that running a freelance business makes sense for your current goals and aspirations. You've learned about the importance of treating your freelance career as a legitimate business, rather than just a "side hobby" that you do for fun. You recognize the wide range of responsibilities that you'll need to manage and you've devised an appropriate business plan, complete with specific time-sensitive goals. You're probably ready to start working.

As with any new venture, it's really easy to get very enthusiastic about freelancing when you are first starting out. However, you'll quickly hit one of the biggest hurdles: finding work. When you have little to no experience in freelancing, next to no portfolio to speak of, and a network of potential clients that is likely two sizes too small, it can be difficult to "land" your first gig. That's understandable, but you have to stick it out and keep your nose to the grindstone.

This chapter will explore several of the main issues you'll encounter when you first start looking for work.

Value Your Work and Charge Accordingly

When you first start out with freelancing, one of the very early questions you'll have to ask yourself has to do with your rate. How much should I charge? If I made X number of dollars an hour at my old desk job, would it be appropriate for me to charge the exact same amount when I start with a freelance business doing similar work? The short answer is no.

Remember that there is a very big difference between billable hours and actual hours worked. A client is not going to pay you for the time to maintain your website, maintain your social media presence, deal with accounting responsibilities, and cold call to find new customers. In the context of your business, though, these are definitely *hours worked*, even if they are not directly *billable* to any one client in particular. It's going to take some time for you to figure out the most appropriate rate and it does take some trial and error.

And so, it's important you **keep accurate records**. For my part, I found that it was really helpful to log every hour that I worked each day during my first few months of operation. This helped me figure out how much time I was "working" on my business, how much time I spent each day in billable hours, and how much time it took for me to complete each assignment. Based on this information (and your annual income goals broken down into monthly, weekly, and daily goals), you can work out the rate that you should be charging.

But I'm just starting out. I can't charge my full rate right away, can I?

Make no mistake. The early weeks and months can be very challenging. You can really struggle with finding clients for any number of different reasons. Because of this, many first-time freelancers find themselves offering substantial discounts — working for a pittance, really — so that they can "build a portfolio" and get "more exposure" online and offline.

I've heard of first-time freelancers writing 500-word articles for a couple of dollars each. These articles may take upwards of an hour each to write. Do you really want to be billing at just two dollars an hour? I don't think so. It also places a very small value on your work.

If you're not going to value your work, no one else is going to do it for you.

What you do is *valuable* to your clients. Whether you're writing articles or designing websites, your work provides value to your clients and you need to charge accordingly. You wouldn't expect someone who just finished his plumbing apprenticeship to go around fixing washrooms for $2 an hour, would you? You wouldn't expect an attorney to represent his new clients at a dollar or two at a time, right? Your freelance business is no different.

Yes, you may have to take a hit to your income when you first start out. Yes, your hourly rate may be a little lower in the first year or two until you can build a bigger name for yourself. That's true. However, you shouldn't allow yourself to work for a pittance. It not only devalues your work, but it also devalues the work of other people in the same industry. If you're willing to custom design a website for $5, the client will soon expect other designers to do the same. And that's not good for anyone.

Network with Like-Minded Entrepreneurs

I don't remember where I first heard the phrase, but it is something that every work-from-home professional should seriously take to heart. As a freelance writer, designer, consultant, and so on, you run your own business. However, **just because you work *for* yourself doesn't mean that you should work *by* yourself.** No business exists in isolation.

In my experience, I've found that a very large number of my clients have come my way via a referral. Absolutely, some clients find me through social media, search engines, and other marketing efforts, but direct referrals definitely represent an incredibly important aspect of my business. It is through this kind of word-of-mouth and networking that I have been able to grow my freelance writing business. In speaking with other freelancers, I've learned that their experiences have been much the same.

Does this mean that you have to pay for a co-working space so you can develop those kinds of relationships? No, not necessarily, though that is one avenue that you can explore. You can also network online with like-minded entrepreneurs from all around the world, as well as attend local "meet up" events and social gatherings. Make those connections.

For my part, I attend weekly lunches as part of what we call Dot Com Pho (*dotcompho.com*). It started out as a casual gathering of Internet marketing experts and other online entrepreneurs in and around the Vancouver area. That's a part of it, but it also worked out to be a great place to meet new business contacts. I've collaborated with the people I've met through these lunches and several have signed on to be clients, either on one-off projects or on an ongoing basis.

In addition to being a potential source of new client referrals, these networking opportunities also lend themselves to the sharing of knowledge. Perhaps you're a freelance writer who largely specializes in press releases, but you'd like to know more about writing web copy. Connecting with the right copywriter could help you expand your portfolio in that direction. Perhaps you could connect with someone who is better versed in producing professional videos; referrals could happen in both directions there.

Far too many people who enter into the arena of freelancing view other freelancers as their competition. That may be true to a certain extent, but there is much more to be gained by connecting with and learning from your fellow freelancer than there is to be gained by ignoring them.

Be Wary of the Scam Artists

When you first start out, you'll find that one of the most challenging hurdles you'll need to overcome is landing that first client. It is very difficult to attract new customers when you don't already have a brand presence, when you don't already have an existing portfolio, and when you don't already have a network of contacts. That only makes sense.

You may also get disheartened when a prospective client decides to go with someone more experienced or someone who is willing to do the work at a substantially lower rate. It's tough and it can make for a very frustrating beginning to your freelance career. If this continues, you may find yourself willing to take on work that is less than ideal.

However, you have to be really careful when you get into this situation. Far too often, novice freelancers find themselves falling into the trap of "working" for the scam artists. What are some of the warning signs that you should look for?

- **Writing for Exposure**: I will admit that I fell for this scam early on in my career. You'll find a job posting, whether it be on Craigslist or a freelance bidding site like Elance, but it makes no specific mention of any monetary compensation. Instead, the ad will tell you that this "opportunity" gives you a great chance to "expand your portfolio" and get "exposure." More likely than not, this means that you'll be working for free. If it means getting published in the New York Times, then it might be worth it. If it's for some random small-time website, it's probably in your best interest to stay away.

- **The Endless Revision**: This is why it is important to lay out the terms of your arrangement as clearly as possible right from the get-go. It's not uncommon for a client to request some edits to your first draft, but there are some clients who never seem to be satisfied and are always asking for more revisions. Eventually, they may refuse to pay for your "sub-par" work, because they feel (or at least they say they feel) that it didn't live up to their expectations.

- **Unwilling to Prepay**: In an ideal situation, you probably want all of your clients to provide 100% pre-payment for all your work. This isn't always feasible, but you should be able to get a deposit in good faith, especially when it comes to larger projects. If a client refuses to provide any deposit whatsoever, it could mean that he will be less willing to provide the full payment when it is due. You could end up in the endless revision cycle described above, for example. Be careful.

- **Performance-Based Payment**: "I can pay you $X, but only if this article gets on the first page of Digg. Don't worry, though. I have a huge contact list that will get it Dugg in no time. Guaranteed!" I've fallen for this one before too. If payment for your work is conditional, you run a very significant chance of never getting paid at all. Content networks that pay based on page views can be quite iffy too, because they claim that you can make *up to* a certain amount of money, but the average submission makes *much* less than that.

- **Bait and Switch**: This client will get you to agree to work for them, based on some glowing conditions. They'll give you a full byline, plenty of pre-payment, ad revenue sharing, and all sorts of other good things. Then, they'll turn around and say there was a "misunderstanding" and that you don't actually get all of these perks. The bait and switch is one of the oldest tricks in the book.

- **Uncommon Payment Scheme**: You can take payment from clients from a variety of different means. PayPal is quite common. For larger jobs, you might take a wire transfer. Some people are comfortable with Western Union Money Transfers or ePassporte. That's fine. However, a client who insists on using some sort of payment system that is unfamiliar to you could prove to be trouble. Do your research.

- **Pay to Apply**: You are providing work — whether it be articles, artwork, or coding — for your clients, not the other way around. If they require you to pay a fee to gain access to a job database, stay away. If they require you to pay a fee so that you can start working for them, stay away. By and large, if you need to *pay* anything to take on the project (aside from your own basic needs like software and computer equipment), you should probably stay away.

- **Too Specific a Writing Sample**: It's not out of the ordinary for a client to request a writing sample. That makes sense, because they want to know what you can do. However, when a client asks for a very specific writing sample on a very specific topic, it could be that they are simply looking for some "free" work from you, not hiring you for any project after the sample has been received.

- **Targeting Casual Writers**: Have you ever seen a posting that says the gig is perfect for students, work at home moms, or new writers? There's a reason. They're looking for someone who is willing to take considerably less pay for considerably more work. You might make this sacrifice early on just to build up your portfolio, but it is in your best interest in the long run only to take on work with fair compensation. This is similar to descriptions that call for "no experience necessary."

- **No Company Website**: Is your client only using a Hotmail address to keep in contact with you? Does he not provide you with any company website information whatsoever? That's a bad sign. Unless it is someone who is truly operating as an individual (e.g., wanting a memoir to be written about his grandfather's life), the client should have a company website of some kind where you can do a little background research.

- **Incredibly Vague Description**: The best job descriptions are the most specific ones. They'll outline exactly what is expected of you, what sort of work you're going to be doing, and how you are going to be compensated. Remarkably vague job descriptions leave you with a lot of questions and a lot of cause for concern. If the prospective client doesn't have adequate answers to these questions, you likely should not proceed any further.
- **Too Good to Be True**: And this is pretty much the catch-all. If the job description sounds too good to be true, it probably is. That's the biggest red flag for any scam artist.

Just as you should be careful of the scam artists when buying and selling things on Craigslist or eBay, you should be even more wary of the scam artists when it comes to your freelance work. If you're unsure and would rather not take the gamble, don't do it.

Decide on a Niche or Choose to Diversify

Before you even set out in search of your first freelance gig, you have to ask yourself a very important question: are you going to be a specialist or a generalist? Naturally there are pros and cons to either approach.

Let's start with the path of the specialist. Using the example of a freelance writer, there are some clear advantages to deciding on a very specific niche. When you focus on just one industry and with only one type of writing, you have a much easier time developing your status as an expert in that field.

It almost becomes a self-fulfilling prophecy. The more you focus on this particular niche, the more practice you get, and presumably, the better you will get at your job. Let's say that you choose to specialize in writing press releases for technology companies. The more you do this, the more familiar you will get with the format, the terminology, and what kind of phrasing seems to bring about the greatest success. You can really establish yourself as an expert and you can become the "go to" person for that kind of writing.

On the other hand, focusing on just one niche and one kind of writing will clearly limit your opportunities. Going back to the example of the press release writer, you will then forgo opportunities to write for corporate blogs, white papers, e-books, and all sorts of other kinds of writing. You may even decide against doing press releases outside of a certain industry, further limiting the scope of the writing services that you offer. In this way, there may be times when you are hard-pressed to find work that fits within the strict confines of your niche.

Flipping over to the other side, there are some advantages to being a generalist. When you are a so-called jack of all trades, it is much easier to market yourself to the widest variety of clients, taking on the widest variety of work. One of the greatest strengths to being a generalist is adaptability. Should one niche start to shrink, you can quickly adapt to another niche and continue making money.

Just as it is oftentimes in your best interest to diversify your investment portfolio, you may also want to diversify your investment of time in your freelance business. Write everything from e-books to press releases, website copy to internal communications. This diverse product portfolio allows you to take on a range of projects. It also makes your day-to-day more interesting, because you are tackling a different challenge each day.

However, just as being a specialist has its down sides, so does being a generalist. By spreading yourself too thin across so many different niches, styles, and industries, you'll have a more difficult time selling yourself as an "expert" in any given field. This is not unlike the scenario you find with lawyers, doctors, and any other profession. Brain surgeons earn more money than general practitioners. Attorneys who focus on one kind of law can usually charge more for their work.

The old saying just might hold true. You can become a jack of all trades, but you'll also become a master of none.

At the end of the day, it really boils down to your own personal situation, your personal characteristics, and your personal preferences. Some freelancers thrive as specialists, but just as many are able to find a great deal of success as generalists. The good news is, because you own and run your own business, you can try your hand at both approaches and see which fits your needs best.

Discover Your Most Valuable Resource

The question that just about every beginning freelancer asks is how he or she should go about finding work. This is easily the biggest stumbling block that you will face early in your career and it's the stumbling block that causes many a freelancer to abandon the craft and rejoin the conventional workforce. However, you'll soon discover that the more you stick with it, the better the situation can become.

No, I am not trying to imply that working as a freelance writer is all about rainbows and unicorns. It's still hard work and it still requires a good deal of dedication. However, you will find that certain aspects can become easier over time. And while your skills and perseverance are going to be integral to your success, they may not even be your most valuable resource. So, what is?

When it comes to finding and sustaining a suitable level of "work" for you to do, you'll soon discover that your most valued resource is your existing client base. It's almost ironic, really. In order to find and maintain your target income goals, you'll learn that keeping a customer around is far more valuable than trying to find a new one. This is a mantra and lesson that has been going around the business community for quite some time.

Think about this for a moment.

First, your existing clients already have a good idea of what you can do, how well you are able to do it, and the kind of logistics that they can expect along the way. You've already worked out a payment schedule that works for both of you. You've already developed a workflow that both of you can use. So, even if a client decides to hire you for just a "one-off" project, he or she is much more likely to "re-hire" for a future project than a brand new client altogether.

Have you written a press release for a certain company in the past? Don't be afraid to follow up with this client, even immediately afterward, to see if there is any other work that they would like you to do. Perhaps they want to keep you on board as their "go to" person for press releases. If you're more of a generalist, perhaps you could tell them that you are available for other corporate communications, website copy, marketing materials, and so on.

These ongoing relationships can quickly turn what would have otherwise been a single project for a single fee into a long-term arrangement with a continuous queue of work for you to do. That sure beats spending all the time sending out query letters, seeking out job posts, and cold-calling potential clients.

Earlier in this book, I discussed the importance of networking with like-minded entrepreneurs. This networking can open up a world of opportunities for you, because it allows you to connect with people, companies, and industries that you may not have otherwise. The exact same philosophy applies when it comes to your existing client base.

Believe it or not, your clients don't live or work in isolation. They interact with other people and companies too. As a result, it's not difficult to give that gentle nudge, telling clients that should any of their other colleagues or acquaintances need some work done, they should be telling these colleagues about you. These "word of mouth" referrals can quickly become the lifeblood of your business. Remember that. It can become positively crucial to your long-term viability and success.

Chapter 3: Managing and Expanding Your Business

Many people seem to enter the arena of freelancing with a fairly simplistic view of what that decision really constitutes. As a freelance designer, someone might assume that several hours will be spent designing a variety of website layouts, company logos, and other graphic elements. As a freelance writer, someone might assume that all you need to do is to be a good writer. For better or for worse, there's so much more to it.

You'll quickly discover the many different hats that you'll need to wear over the course of your freelance career, because you'll quickly learn that you aren't *just* a writer or *just* a designer; you are a small business owner. As such, there are many concerns and issues that will arise as you learn how to manage and expand your business. Many of the challenges very much have their parallels in the realm of traditional brick-and-mortar businesses, but they can also be unique to the perspective of a freelancer.

Here are five major lessons to take to heart when it comes to the daily operations of your business, as well as the development of opportunities for growth moving forward.

Keep Accurate and Up-to-Date Records of Everything

When you're ready to hurl yourself headlong into the world of freelancing, you may get excited by the prospect of drumming up new clients or working on that first project. That's great. That kind of enthusiasm is a very powerful thing, but something that you'll need to establish right from the get-go is a good record keeping system.

This is a business and it needs to be treated as such. It's up to you find the system that best suits your preferences and your way of doing things, but you'll want to keep track of all your client projects, the in-flow and out-flow of money, and anything else that may relate to your business. You'll want to have reminders in place, for example, that tell you it's time to renew the domain name for your business website.

Speaking for myself, most of my accounting and bookkeeping is still done with Microsoft Excel. I have put together spreadsheet templates that work well for me, so I haven't yet found the need to invest in invoicing software or CRM software. Depending on your circumstances and the nature of your business, it may make more sense to use a different kind of record-keeping solution. Perhaps a database program is better suited for you, for instance.

But it's not enough simply to set up the system and then forget about it. You need to keep it up to date on a regular basis. For me, I update transactions as they happen, but this might not be viable if you're dealing with a lot more. It might be better to set aside an hour or several hours each week where you tally up all the transactions for that previous week. I also find that it's helpful to do a monthly review, going over everything that happened to make sure it's all accurate and complete, as well as to see the overall health of the business.

By keeping up the habit of maintaining your books and keeping them up to date, you make the job a lot easier when it comes to tax season. All the books are already in order, they're already perfectly organized, and they're all ready to be entered into the appropriate tax software. That's great if you're going to do your own taxes and your accountant will love you for these comprehensive records if you choose to hire a professional to handle your taxes instead.

You also have to remember that good records go beyond just accounting too.

If you have a large client base, it may be worthwhile to invest in a CRM solution that helps you better manage that Rolodex, as well as keep tabs on client preferences. Relying on your very fallible human memory is incredibly unreliable. Does this client prefer images to be saved in JPG or PNG format? Was this the client that wanted <h2> subject headings or <h1> subject headings in the WordPress blog posts? What was the agreed upon word count again? Some of these can be managed with another spreadsheet or database. Just choose a system that you know will work for you *and one that you'll actually use and update.*

Similarly, if your projects tend to be longer in nature, consisting of multiple parts and possibly involving collaboration with multiple people, it may also be useful to invest in project management software to keep better records of everything to do with those projects too. Web-based solutions like Basecamp are particularly powerful.

Keep records of everything. You'll save yourself *a lot* of headache down the road.

Maintain an Online Presence with Blogs and Social Media

The Internet is a vast and varied place. As such, it can be increasingly difficult to stand out from the crowd. Even if you have designed and developed a fantastic website for your freelance business, it's not going to do you any good if no one knows it is there.

Yes, proper marketing and search engine optimization will certainly play their respective roles, but it is equally important that you pay attention to social media as well. These social networking channels give you the opportunity to engage with your potential clients, as well as people who may refer you to people who can become your customers.

When you build that presence and build that following, people in and out of your niche are much more likely to know who you are and what you have to offer. They're much more likely to understand what expertise and skills you bring to the table and, more importantly, they're much more likely to find you.

The social networks you use will depend somewhat on your industry and who you believe to be your ideal client.

- Mainstays like Facebook, Twitter, and LinkedIn are great places to start, connecting with people who can serve as your ambassadors.

- YouTube is a fantastic way to build up your video marketing efforts, reaching a global audience in a very effective way.
- Pinterest is gaining in popularity, applicable to a wide range of industries and interests.
- If you're a photographer, networks like 500px and Flickr are terrific venues to showcase your work to potential clients, encouraging them to hire you for their own projects.
- If you're more of a graphic artist, perhaps deviantART is worth exploring.

Another strategy to consider is adding a blog to your site. You can install WordPress in a manner of minutes, customizing it to suit your particular preferences and needs. Having a blog serves several purposes.

- It gives you the opportunity to establish yourself as an expert. It's one thing to talk the talk, but the blog is a platform where you can show clients that you actually walk the walk.
- It allows you to showcase and promote your work. If you're a writer, the blog functions as an ongoing portfolio. If you're a photographer or artist, you can highlight some of your recent work or discuss some of the techniques you use.
- It makes your site dynamic. By having new content posted all the time, this indicates to search engines

like Google that they should be indexing your site more often. This helps with search rankings and the relative "importance" that search engines place on your site.

- It gives you a reason to share. While you could send out links to your services or portfolio page on Twitter, having new posts on your blog gives you a legitimate reason to send out those tweets or Facebook updates. New and returning visitors can then further explore your site and see what you have to offer.

If you want to attract business, you must first get noticed and you must retain that attention. Social media and blogs are tools that can be used to achieve those goals.

Establish Yourself as an Expert

They say that variety is the spice of life, but diversifying your service offerings as a freelancer may not be the best path to prosperity. I do enjoy varying up my projects from time to time, but it is absolutely true that specialists can charge more for their work than generalists, precisely because the specialists bring an extra level of specific expertise to the table.

A general photographer may be able to charge one set of fees, but the photographer with a set of skills (and a portfolio) perfectly suited for wedding shoots has better earning potential. The same can be said about the writer who specializes in press releases for pharmaceutical companies, for example, as those clients will seek out this professional specifically for that purpose. This can limit your potential client base, but the right clients will more than make up for it.

So, what can you do to build that reputation as an expert in your field?

- Participate in social media. As I said in the previous section, social media is a great way to build brand awareness, letting people know who you are and what you do. They'll come to know you as "the writer who knows everything about (fill in the blank)."
- Run a business blog. I also mentioned this in the previous section. Using a blog for your freelance

business, you can demonstrate your specific expertise in that field. If you're a financial advisor, educate the public about some of the important laws or forms that might interest them. You're still valued for your individualized advice, but you show that you know your stuff.

- Author a book. While you may or may not make money from the book directly, you will get the indirect benefit of improved legitimacy in your field. This is partly why I co-authored Make Money Online: Roadmap of a Dot Com Mogul with John Chow. Some people already knew me as a professional blogger; the book helped to solidify that perception.
- Speak at events. You could run a workshop, host a lecture, or be a guest speaker at someone else's event. Again, this helps to solidify your reputation. I was a featured lunch speaker at Freelance Camp Vancouver 2010, for example, where I talked about why all freelancers should have a blog.
- Solicit interviews. This is another way to get out in the public eye. I've been interviewed by The Commentary on several occasions, demonstrating my expertise in professional blogging, cell phones, consumer electronics, social media, and more.

To be fair, there is definitely value in expanding beyond your niche too. I do it all the time, because it helps to keep those writing skills fresh and sharp. As with all other things in life, it's about balance.

Realize No Pond Is Too Big for Your Small Fish

They say that you'll never know what is possible unless you strive for what is impossible. Actor Will Smith once said, "The most common road to mediocrity is being realistic." The goal that you'll never achieve is the one that you never set out for yourself in the first place, thinking that it was utterly out of reach.

And it is this kind of mentality that keeps many freelancers in a relative state of stagnation and complacency. They figure that they're only a small fish and, as such, can only swim around in small ponds. They don't take the chance of going after the bigger fish in the bigger pond, because they don't think that they can compete. But how can they know that?

Yes, it is probably true that the average freelance writer won't get his or her article featured on the front page of the New York Times, but the average freelance writer doesn't submit his or her article to the New York Times either. If you don't try, you don't succeed. If you try and you happen to get that feature article published, you may lay a path for massive opportunities moving forward.

It's going to take persistence and hard work. No one said it was going to be easy. You'll have to endure through rejection letters and non-responses, but this is the only way that you give yourself a chance at a breakthrough moment. Actors, singers, artists, photographers, designers, authors... many of the greatest emerged from obscurity because they took that chance and they got noticed.

Perhaps you're not comfortable with that quantum leap. If that's the case, try broadening your scope and expanding your business in phases. Go after the client that you think is just outside of your reach, the contact that is just a little beyond your sphere. With each successive expansion, you'll get bigger and gain confidence.

Then, you can really go after the big fish and demonstrate that you belong.

Be Crystal Clear with Rate Quotes and Requirements

"How much do you charge for blogging?"

I can't even begin to count the number of e-mails I've received where that is the entirety of the message body. The trouble with such a simple request is that putting together a rate quote can be a much more complex process that takes in many more factors. You may be thinking one thing, but your potential client could be thinking something else entirely.

Let's say, hypothetically, that I were to reply to this e-mail by stating that I charge $50 for a blog post. In my mind, I may be thinking that the post will be no more than 250 words and that it will require virtually no research whatsoever. I may be thinking that I will receive a full byline credit (By Michael Kwan), complete with a link back to my website. I may think that all they want is plain text with no formatting and no images. I may think that they don't require any additional support or services from me aside from the raw text.

And then, continuing with this hypothetical example, I come to learn that the client had an entirely different notion of the type of blogging he required. Maybe he was expecting a post of at least 1,500 words. Maybe he was expecting extensive online and offline research. Maybe he was expecting that there is no difference between a byline and complete ghostwriting. Maybe he was expecting the post to be fully formatted in HTML and that it would include several unique images. Maybe he expects that I will promote the post, for free, through the various social media and social bookmarking networks.

You can see how this can quickly become a very ugly situation.

It's even worse when you get asked how much you charge for "articles" or something even more vague. Blogging on the Internet is quite different from producing a feature article for a print magazine, writing a press release, or putting together a technical document for a very esoteric audience.

When you provide a rate quote on any given project, you should be absolutely crystal clear about what that price includes (and what it doesn't include). These factors can be just as important as the actual dollar amount.

Some questions you may want to ask yourself and your client include the following:

- Will you be offering revisions if the original draft is not satisfactory?
- What kind of writing is required?
- What is the estimated word count?
- Is this a one-time project or is there an ongoing commitment?

- What is the expected monthly volume for an ongoing commitment?
- Is this on a ghostwriting basis or will full credit be given?
- How much research and guidance will be provided?
- What is the budget?
- Who is the audience?
- What is the expected timeline for delivery?
- What are the payment terms?

There are many more questions that you can ask too. Knowing the location (for legal purposes) of your client is important when it comes to charging sales tax, for example.

Don't make assumptions. A client may see that you are very active in social media and simply assume that you will "tweet" out a link to every article that you post on the Internet. Conversely, you may assume that your client will want no more than one or two revisions, but somehow you get pulled into an endless back-and-forth with edit after edit after edit. Be clear from the beginning so there are no misinterpretations later on.

After all, you wouldn't walk into a car dealership and ask, "How much is a car?" There are many different cars, all with different features, benefits, and selling points... and different prices, warranties, and service plans. Part of your job as a freelancer is to match up the right "car" to fit your customer's needs, desires and budget.

Chapter 4: Dealing with the Day-to-Day Grind

The early days in your freelancing career will likely see their fair share of frustrations, especially when it comes to learning the ropes and trying to land more projects, but you'll likely approach these challenges with a good deal of enthusiasm. This is an exciting new venture and you're committed to giving it 110%. That's great. However, like all other things, the honeymoon period eventually ends and you can find yourself in quite a slump.

Don't get me wrong. I love the lifestyle that running a freelance writing business affords me, but it is certainly not without its difficulties. In this chapter, we'll explore some strategies for keeping things fresh and for maintaining a healthy life-work balance. This is particularly difficult if this is your first experience working from a home office. You'll want to maintain a high level of enthusiasm throughout your career too, so it's important to know how to do that.

Take Well-Deserved Breaks as Needed

Many have said that one of the biggest drawbacks to being a work-at-home entrepreneur is that you will be prone to burnout. It's inevitable, no matter how much you love what you do or how goal-oriented you happen to be. As you will be working out of a home office and there is no set work schedule, it becomes seemingly impossible to separate work and play. Where is the division between your professional life and your personal life? How do you manage to stay as productive as possible without wanting to tear your arm out of its socket?

Speaking for myself, one way that I keep productive is to take on a number of varied projects. This way, I don't pigeon-hole myself. I do both freelance writing for a niche and for the masses; by keeping the variety up, I can largely manage to keep things fresh as a freelance writer. Even so, I do hit a brick wall from time to time, no matter how motivated I am to get things done that day, that week, or that month.

So, just as you would with a regular 9-to-5 kind of job, you have to remember to take well-deserved breaks from your work. The emphasis here is on *well-deserved*. If you find yourself slacking off all the time, playing Farmville instead of putting fingers to keyboard, you don't deserve a break. If you find yourself chatting with friends on instant messenger rather than researching the information you need for that new project, you don't deserve a break. However, if you've been tracking your hours (and dollars earned) and you see that you've reasonably accomplished your goals for the week, taking a lazy Friday is perfectly acceptable.

Go ahead. Get out there and experience the real world.

A big problem with working from home is that you are never really off the clock. You may feel that because you *can* work at any hour of the day that you *should* work at every hour of every day. That's just not healthy. For some of us, overcoming that sense of guilt can be quite the hurdle and that's why we have to convince ourselves that a break really is in our best interest.

Sometimes, the best thing you can do to improve your productivity is to stop working, if only for half an hour at a time. Spending hours on end staring at a computer monitor isn't going to do you much good if your writing quality suffers. The same is true with photo editing, graphic design, app coding or any number of similar tasks.

Your clients deserve better than that. You deserve better than that. When your brain is turning to mush, as it inevitably will after an extended work session, it means that you need to leave the computer and do something else. Go stretch. Go play some video games. Go read a book.

Again, I have to emphasize that these must be *well-deserved breaks* and not just breaks. After a few minutes away from the keyboard, you can return refreshed, recharged, and sharper than ever. This is why many high-stress, high-volume jobs (casino dealer, customs officer, and so on) require their employees to take frequent breaks. It helps with their concentration and it helps them do their job better. The same is true with your career.

Go for a Walk and Socialize with Real People

This goes hand-in-hand with the previous tip. Working from home as a freelance writer, I spend the majority of my day staring at the same four walls (or at the same computer monitor) for hours at a time. I'm thankful that I have a dedicated home office that provides some separation between what is work and what is home, but since I am "at the office" alone for most hours of the day, it can get very quiet.

And having my thoughts echo between my ears probably isn't the healthiest thing in the world either.

Human beings are inherently social animals and even if you are more on the introverted end of the spectrum, you need to be around people from time to time. This is particularly true if you're coming from a more traditional work environment where you can gossip with your colleagues or chat with your customers.

One option is to consider coworking. Many major cities have coworking offices set up where you can get a dedicated space that is always yours or you can book a desk on an as-needed basis. In the Vancouver area where I am, one of the best coworking options is with The Network Hub. They offer conference room rentals, hotdesking services, mailbox rentals and other related services too. Whatever you choose, a coworking configuration can surround you with typically like-minded entrepreneurs who may be facing the same challenges as you. It can also give you some great networking opportunities to share referrals and business all around.

If you're like me and you still prefer the home office environment, this still means that you need to go outside and see the real world. It is of paramount importance to breathe some fresh air each and every day, as well as interact with some real people. Get a little human interaction. This could be as simple as grabbing a coffee at the local cafe or visiting the local grocer to pick up some supplies. Maybe when you go out to grab the newspaper, you'll bump into your neighbor and have a nice chat.

Even if you don't *talk* to anyone else, just being around people will help to remind you of what it means to be human. There is a real world beyond the Internet, believe it or not.

Another major benefit to going outside is that you can get away from that stagnant home office air. It can get pretty stuffy, so taking a brief stroll around the neighborhood lets you stretch your legs, get some exercise, and breathe in some fresh air. It can be very refreshing. Sitting at a desk all day can wreak havoc on your back, your posture and your hips too. That walk, while not being quite enough for a full exercise routine, certainly doesn't hurt.

We all need breaks. While you may want to be as productive as possible and just pound away at that keyboard all day, you will actually be more productive if you take a break from time to time. This lets you recharge the batteries and refresh the mind. It can also present you with an opportunity to develop some new ideas that can then be implemented in an article, in your business, or in whatever else you do. Fresh ideas come from a fresh mind, not a tired and weary one.

Learn Something New Every Day

There is definitely something to be said about finding your stride. It can feel like a great thing when you find your groove, gaining the ability to almost work on autopilot. However, when you're in business for yourself as a freelancer, this "autopilot" experience can get very boring very quickly. When the work starts to feel too routine, it may not excite you anymore. It may not invigorate you. It may not motivate you. And then you won't want to do it anymore.

This is why I try to make it a point to learn something new every day. It doesn't have to be something particularly monumental, like learning a brand new programming language or figuring out how another content management system works. While it would ideally be relevant to your line of work, providing you with some way of expanding your business and growing your revenue, learning something completely off the wall can be useful too.

If nothing else, it will help to keep your mind fresh. The brain is like any other muscle. It needs exercise in order for it to stay healthy, but going through exactly the same exercise routine each and every day is only going to tire out one part while under-developing other parts. Shake things up. An active mind helps you stay and feel younger.

In the context of being a writer, learning something new has an additional benefit: it helps to expand my knowledge base.

What this means is that the next time I have a client who wants to me write about topic X, I may be better prepared with more background knowledge in that arena. This saves research time and I become a more valuable resource for my clients. The work is better. They're happier and I'm happier. Everyone wins.

This also helps to bolster your creativity, which is of critical importance to anyone working in a creative field. You could be a photographer, a graphic artist, a copywriter, or a documentary filmmaker. Whatever the case, expanding your knowledge and having these little tidbits and facts in the back of your mind can help to provide much needed inspiration and guidance.

You are in a knowledge-based economy. Build up your savings.

Find Your Personal Source of Motivation

When you're working for someone else in a more conventional office job, you can have some assurance that your day will start at a certain time and it will end at a certain time. This isn't always the case, but you generally know when you are "on the clock." The same does not apply when you get yourself into the world of freelancing, particularly if you work from home, because you could theoretically work at any hour of the day.

That may sound great at first, but it quickly turns into a double-edged sword. You are effectively giving yourself a perpetual excuse to procrastinate. I don't *have to* write this article right now and I don't *have to* finish this web design right this moment, because I *can* do it later. To this end, one of the biggest challenges that you are going to face as a work-from-home entrepreneur is finding a personal source of motivation. What can you do to get yourself started? What can you do to keep working when you may rather do something else?

Going back for a moment to the context of working a more conventional office job, that "inspiration" or "motivation" might come simply because you have a supervisor, manager, or some other authority figure looming over your shoulder. He or she may hound you if you don't complete your assigned tasks. If you don't do your job and do it well, you'll probably get disciplined, formally or informally.

But what about when you freelance? Without someone hounding you for eight hours a day, five days a week, the only person to keep you on track *is you*. Sure, a big part of the motivation comes from the simple fact that if you don't work, you don't get paid, but it runs far deeper than that. And so, you need to develop methodologies that will keep you on track. Here are a few strategies that have worked for me.

- **Track Your Work Time:** Yes, you will need to keep track of your contracts, income and expenses for accounting purposes, but there is more here when it comes to the issue of motivation (or lack thereof). The record-keeping can go beyond dollars and cents. Instead, you can log your hours. Yes, while you should work *smarter* rather than *harder*, time is one of the best quantitative measures you can use for how much work you're actually accomplishing. I'm not talking about simply tracking how much time you spend at your office; rather, track the time that you are actually *working*. You might be surprised by how much time you are wasting with procrastination and distraction. When you know that you are effectively observing yourself and your habits, you are more likely to stay on task.

- **Set 3 x 3 Monetary Goals:** You are already tracking your income, but have you broken down these figures in terms of when you are earning them? This will vary based on the kind of work you do and how you get paid, but you might want to see how much you are making each day, each week, and each month. This is not to say that you take your monthly income and divide it by the number of working days, but rather to see how much you earned on that specific day. The system that I used for the longest time consisted of a 3x3 matrix. On one axis, I put daily, weekly and monthly timelines. On the other axis, I put a minimum, expected and ideal goal. This results in nine numbers and it gives you a sense of where you are. You want to make sure that you always hit the minimum goal, no matter what, and you'd like to hit the expected goal on a fairly regular basis. If you hit that ideal goal, reward yourself accordingly.

- **Leverage Self-Imposed Incentives:** Many people derive their motivation from keeping the end goal in mind. The problem is that the "real" rewards—like completing a large project or receiving a massive royalty payment—may not be frequent enough to keep you motivated in the long term. While long-term goals and long-term rewards absolutely have value, you may also consider dangling a carrot that's a little more within reach. You need to acknowledge your success in the short term. Provide yourself with some self-defined incentives for the short-term. Tell yourself that if you are able to complete task X within a timeframe of Y, then you will be rewarded with Z.

It's really up to you what you want to use as a reward. Sometimes, something as simple as saying that you can log off from the computer and enjoy a work-free weekend with the family can be motivation enough.

- **Employ a False Sense of Urgency:** Someone once said that there is nothing more motivating than an imminent deadline. You've likely experienced a variation of this while going through school. Your teacher assigns an essay to you that is due in a month. You figure you have a month, so you put it off. And off. And off. Then, all of a sudden, the whole month passes you by and the essay is due tomorrow. Somehow, you miraculously put in the hard work with an all-nighter and the essay gets written. It may not be your best work, but it got done. While I certainly don't recommend you utilize this strategy too often, employing a false sense of urgency works. This forces you out of the habit of procrastination and kicks you into gear *right now.* Manifest an artificial deadline for the project, so that it feels like it needs to be done right this instant. For example, I may force myself to complete an article for a client before I go to bed that night, even if the client doesn't really *need* it right away. If you get into the habit of always putting things off, you will build up an ever-expanding backlog. Creating these deadlines reduces the possibility of that happening and, thus, you are able to stay on track and keep up with current projects.

- **Challenge Your Colleagues:** Just because you work *for* yourself doesn't mean that you need to work *by* yourself. In fact, working *with* other freelancers and entrepreneurs can be a great motivating factor. On the one hand, you can think of them as rivals. Would Magic Johnson have achieved the same kind of success if it were not for Larry Bird? They may feel like they have something to prove and they use their rival as a measuring stick. Bragging rights and self-satisfaction go a long way. At the same time, you can also find motivation with someone who you consider to be a colleague or a peer. You feel good when you see your colleague succeed and he feels the same in kind when you manage to achieve something. This is the exact same idea as having a workout buddy for your exercise routine, because you are there to keep one another in check. When partner A isn't feeling particularly motivated, partner B can keep partner A accountable. They can encourage one another, achieving greater things together than they may have achieved individually. There can be some healthy competition here: if your partner runs the 100-meter dash in 12 seconds, you're much more motivated to do it in 10 seconds.

Many people, when they first start out with their respective freelance careers, will be highly motivated. They'll approach this new endeavor with a great deal of enthusiasm and energy, but that can easily wane over time. When you get waist-deep in the grind of daily operations, it can be challenging to maintain those high spirits and that's why finding ongoing and persistent sources of personal motivation is so important. You have to find what will keep you going, even when you hit some rough patches... or writer's block.

Invest in Relevant Equipment and Business Expenses

This will definitely vary depending on the type of work that you do, but it is generally true that you can get started with freelancing with a very small budget. Speaking from my experience as a freelance writer, all I really needed was a reliable computer, a reliable Internet connection, and a comfortable space to do my work. I already had a computer, my home already had Internet access, and I already had a perfectly usable desk. Along the way, you may accrue some other expenses like registering a domain for your website and buying some web hosting.

Indeed, this is one of the major reasons why someone may choose to try freelancing in the first place. The startup costs are generally far lower than opening up a traditional brick-and-mortar business. Photographers may need to invest in some camera equipment and graphic designers may need some software, but if they're considering these options as a freelance career, there's a good chance that they've already gotten started down that path. It's likely that they want to convert a hobby into a business; I know that's how I got started with writing professionally.

That being said, it is still important to treat your freelance business *as a business*. What this means is that when it does become necessary to purchase some equipment or buy some software, you do it and you think of it as an investment. The same can be said about paying for professional services, because of cost, time and quality.

A prime example of this is a business card. You may think that you're doing the majority of your communication online—and that could be true—but having a professional business card really helps to legitimize in-person interactions. Business cards are relatively inexpensive to print and there are many online and offline vendors for this. But it's not just about the printing; it's also about the design.

Yes, you could try to fumble your way through some unfamiliar design software to create your own business card, but I don't recommend this. First, you'll probably take far longer to come up with a reasonable design than someone who does this kind of designing for a living. Second, the design that you create probably won't be as good as the one the professional creates either. I'm not saying you should break the bank on the most expensive graphic designer out there, but be willing to pay for quality. You'd expect the same from your clients, right?

Speaking for myself, my original business card design was created by a professional for about $200. She vectorized my logo, provided me with all the graphics, and even gave me the Adobe Illustrator file in case I wanted to make any edits myself. I then proceeded to print a batch of about 1000 business cards for about $200. I'm reasonably confident that I have recouped that $400, but looking back, I may have been able to save a little money here and there. Even so, I viewed it as an investment and it has paid off in the long run.

The same can be said about other professional services you may need, like web design, accounting, dealing with income taxes, social media management, and so forth.

Similarly, while your focus will mostly be on the actual work that you do for your clients, you will also need to think about your personal logistics and equipment needs. Do you have a good, comfortable office chair? Do you have a multifunction printer with scanning capabilities? Is your computer adequate for the work that you need to do? I reiterate that you shouldn't be irresponsible with your business spending just because you can "write it off," but you should be willing to invest in your business where it makes sense.

Chapter 5: Moving Toward Greater Independence

Perhaps it's because you found that traditional office politics didn't work for you. Perhaps you didn't like the power dynamic or you simply didn't like having a boss loom over your shoulder. Whatever the case, you decided that you want to head out on your own and become a freelancer. And the most important part of that word, freelancer, is "free."

You want to be free. You want to be in control. You want to be your own boss.

My hope is that the previous four chapters have helped to better prepare you for the life of a freelancer, giving you some of the tools that you'll need to get started, to find clients, and to make the most of your daily operations. Moving forward, though, you may become increasingly motivated to seek even greater independence. In this fifth and final chapter, we will explore some key concepts that will lead you down that path, allowing you to truly work on your own terms and achieve both greater success and greater freedom.

Stop Wishing and Start Doing

I wish I could afford to have dinner at the swankiest restaurant in town. I wish I didn't have to endure the hour-long commute to the office every morning. I wish my life was easier and not filled with all these stresses, concerns, and problems.

Do any of these statements sound familiar? Do you find yourself engaging in a similar kind of negative self-talk, feeling a little disdain for your current existence and yearning for the greener pastures that are surely on the other side of the seemingly unattainable fence? You're not alone. It is a natural part of the human condition to want more, to want better, and to want it now. That's normal.

However, wishing won't get you anywhere. All wishing will foster is a greater sense of disdain, futility, and further inferiority. What you need to do is to stop wishing and to start doing.

This very much applies to the world of freelancing, especially when you are first starting out. You could wish to attract more clients, to make more money and to have more flexibility in your schedule, but nothing is going to change and nothing is going to happen unless you take action. If you want to achieve greater success and enjoy greater freedom, then you have to be prepared to work for it and you need to put a plan of action into place.

At some point during my university career, I decided that I may be interested in becoming a professional writer. I wished that I could pursue this interest and be compensated fairly for it, earning a reasonable income doing what I love to do. Rather than sit around and continue to wish for this to happen, I took action.

While still in university, I maintained my own website where I wrote articles periodically. I also wrote for a friend's website and signed on as a contributing writer for a student newsletter. Upon graduation, I applied for nearly any position that was remotely related to writing as a career. I eventually found myself writing and editing for a local Buddhist organization, helping them clean up their Chinese-to-English translations so that they'd be more palatable for a North American audience. I'm not exactly a Buddhist, I can't read Chinese, and it wasn't exactly what I had in mind, but it was a start.

From there, I developed an interest in freelancing, looking for potential opportunities online. I found my first couple of clients and everything snowballed from there. Had I not started writing for my own website, had I not volunteered for the student newsletter, had I not taken that position at the Buddhist organization, I may not be where I am today. Now, I get to write about topics that interest me and while I don't consider myself rich, I am being compensated fairly for my work and I am able to make a living doing this.

I'd be more successful if only I were born into a wealthier, better connected family. I'd be more successful if I were not the youngest in the family. I'd be in better physical shape if I could afford to eat healthier foods on a more consistent basis. What do all these statements have in common? They place the speaker in the position of the victim. It's not my fault, right?

Wrong.

The longer that you assert that you are the victim of the situation, the greater the sense of helplessness and lack of control that you will start to feel. This is not the position that you want find yourself. Instead, take the proactive position and make your life what you want it to be. Stop wishing and start doing. Start setting goals and establishing plans of action for how you want to achieve those goals.

It's good to have wishes and it's good to have dreams, as these can help to define the road map that you want to take in life. However, without a plan of action and the actual impetus to put those plans into action, your wishes and dreams will remain just that: wishes and dreams.

As a freelance photographer, do you wish that you'd get featured in a photography magazine? As a freelance web designer, do you wish that you could create a stunning new design for a multinational corporation? As a freelance writer, do you wish that you could publish a real physical book and see it in stores?

You'll be setting new and increasingly ambitious goals as your freelance career matures. They may require more effort and the plans may get more complex, but the same lesson still holds true: no matter what you want to achieve, you can. You just have to do something about it.

Gain and Achieve the Freedom of Time

While my career choice as a freelance writer does not offer unicorns and rainbows each and every day, the benefits of this lifestyle far outweigh the shortcomings that come along with it. At least for me. This won't be the case for everyone, because we all have our own individual preferences and desires. Structure can be good sometimes, but freelancing is ultimately about being free. You are free to work where you want, whether that's in a home office, in a coworking space, at the coffee shop, or on a beach in Cancun.

By far the best freedom that comes with freelancing, though, is the freedom of time. Assuming that I partake in a little forethought and planning, I have a much more flexible schedule than if I held a more conventional job with some conventional company. I'm not bound to a 9-to-5 schedule, Monday to Friday, but I can most certainly work during those hours if that's what I want to do. I can take a three hour lunch break most days with no real negative ramifications, as long as I make up those three hours later in the day or week. It is easier for me to accommodate a dentist appointment. It's not that I'm working less than people who have regular jobs; it's just that my schedule is generally more flexible.

So, how do you get there?

It really depends on the kind of work that you take. Speaking for myself, most of the writing projects that I have aren't really bound to a specific time of day. I may have a feature article to write for a website, for example, and it needs to be published some time this week. It doesn't matter if I write this article in the middle of the day, after dinner, or in the wee hours of the night. It just matters if I get the job done and that it's done well.

That's time freedom.

But that's not always the case. I also have ongoing relationships with some clients where I may have some daily obligations. I may be expected to blog daily, reporting on relevant news from the day. I may be expected to monitor their Twitter account for mentions or to moderate comments on their site. This doesn't provide as much time freedom, because I am expected to be available during certain hours of the day.

In order to achieve greater time freedom under these circumstances, some measures can be taken. For example, if I know that I need a day off during the week for some personal commitments, I simply communicate this to the client and make the necessary arrangements. For blogging, I may be able to pre-write the content ahead of time and use the "timestamp" feature in WordPress.

In a more general sense, though, achieving time freedom means that you don't need to request vacation days and wait for approval from a superior. While you can't just pick up and go on a holiday on a moment's notice — you need to prepare for it ahead of time — freelancers do have the relative freedom to create their own schedules. As you approach the time that you'd like to take that well-deserved holiday, you simply stop taking on new projects that could encroach on that timeframe. You simply tell your clients that you won't be available until such-and-such a date.

Having time freedom doesn't mean that you can abandon work altogether. What it does mean is that you have the flexibility to adapt your work schedule to best fit your lifestyle.

You just have to plan ahead.

Continue Working on Your Search Engine Optimization

Every business should have a website and, as a freelancer, you are running a business. As such, it is very important that you maintain at least a simple website where potential clients and partners can find you and learn more about what you have to offer.

On this website, you can introduce yourself, have a page that describes your various services, and have a page that can act as your online portfolio. It's also helpful to have a page with client feedback in the form of testimonials and another page with pertinent contact information. It's really up to you what you want to include, but you really should have that website to establish a "home base" on the Internet that can legitimize your freelance business.

That's great and all, but having a website that no one can find isn't going to be all that useful. While your more active marketing efforts — cold calls, job boards, networking, social media marketing, and so on — may attract a significant number of leads, you also want to make sure that your website is clearly visible online. This means ranking in the search engines for important keywords and keyword phrases.

If you are a freelance event photographer in Toronto, then a keyword term that you may want to target is "Toronto event photographer." If you are first on the list of results, there's a good chance that you are going to attract some good leads that way. This isn't an SEO (search engine optimization) book, so I won't go into the finer details of how you can attempt to rank for your target keyword terms, but it is definitely something that you want to keep in mind long term.

How does this help you achieve greater independence? While your active marketing will continue to play a role, having a website that ranks well can passively generate leads for you. This saves you time and effort in the long run. As you get more leads, you can become increasingly selective with your clients and ultimately earn higher rates as a result. It's simply a matter of supply and demand.

Generate Reliable Sources of Passive Income

As much as you may love what you do, you can't possibly be doing it all of the time. There are only so many hours in the day and as you continue to trade hours for dollars, as it were, you will only generate an income when you are actively working. That's the nature of freelancing, really. If you're a freelance writer, you get paid to write. If you stop writing, you stop earning. If you're a freelance photographer, you get paid to take and edit pictures. If you stop taking photos, you stop getting paid. It's not a business that can run by itself and, as such, it's not a business model that can produce passive income.

But it doesn't have to be that way. Indeed, if you want to achieve a greater level of independence, you will want to consider the possibility of passive income. This way, you can continue earning, even if you aren't actively working. And yes, it is possible to make passive income as a freelance writer; you can write it once and continue earning money for years to come.

The interest that you earn from your savings account at the bank is passive income. After you put that money in there, you don't have to do anything else to earn that interest. You just get some extra spending money each month. The same kind of philosophy can apply, to an extent, to freelancing and there are several ways to go about it.

- **Blogging** - In the strictest sense, blogging isn't really a source of passive income, because there are certain things that you will need to do on an ongoing basis. You will need to continue working on your search engine optimization and you will need to moderate comments and you will need to keep producing new content. That being said, once a blog post is written, it can continue to generate revenue well into the future. Speaking for my own blog, Beyond the Rhetoric (http://btr.michaelkwan.com), much of the traffic that I receive is for older posts in my archive rather than the brand new posts that I publish six times a week. These are typically blog posts that rank well for certain keywords that approach relatively evergreen topics. People are constantly searching for information on the Internet and having that blog post there can help make money even when you're not really doing anything else. And you don't have to be a great writer either, per se, because there are all sorts of profitable photo blogs, online comics, video blogs, graphic design blogs, and more. As an added bonus, your blog can act as a living portfolio or showcase of your work, passively marketing your skills and services to potential clients.
- **Profit Sharing** - In general, freelancers receive a one-time payment for work completed. Writers may get paid per article, photographers may get paid per session, and logo designers may get paid per logo

designed. This helps with predictability, but it does not help with generating a passive income. Another model that you may want to consider as part of your mix is a profit sharing model. It is certainly a gamble to give up on the guaranteed income, so you'll need to weigh your pros and cons carefully before proceeding, but the long-term projection can prove to be quite profitable. Let's say that you are a freelance video production house and you are putting together a documentary DVD for a client. You could set a rate for the project, but you could also say that you want a certain percentage of all sales over the lifetime of the product.

- **Affiliate Marketing** - This will depend heavily on the client and the nature of the work, but there is sometimes the opportunity to make additional money through affiliate marketing. Affiliate marketing is when you get paid a commission if someone completes a certain action or completes a purchase of a product. Amazon has one of the biggest affiliate programs on the Internet. If you sign up and promote certain products, you earn a percentage of all the sales that result from your promotion. In the context of passive income for the freelancer, you may be able to include an affiliate link in your work. For example, when I write a review of a product or service and that review gets published on my client's website, I may request that I can include the affiliate link in the article. When someone reads that review, clicks on the link, and purchases the product, I can earn a commission. If that customer is going to buy that product anyway, I may as well get a piece of the action too.

- **Stock Images and Other Content** - What about all the content that you are not necessarily producing for one specific client? There are many ways that you can capitalize on your skills and talents by selling this content through a variety of online and offline marketplaces. If you are a photographer, you may license your images through services like Corbis, Getty and iStockPhoto. If you are a web designer and coder, you might sell premium WordPress themes and plug-ins. If you are a writer, you may be able to sell premium white papers. Be creative.

These are just a few examples. Passive income really is the best kind of income, because it allows you to continue making money without putting in any additional work or effort. This can provide you with more free time to spend with your family and to do the things that you love to do. This frees up your time to work on personal projects… which just might be the best way to earn an ongoing passive income.

And that leads us right into our next topic.

Transition Toward Selling Products

Yes, the vast majority of your freelance work is going to be for your clients. That only makes sense, because they are paying for your professional services. However, as discussed in these past few sections, you only have so many hours in the day and trading your services for pay necessarily limits your earning potential. While you can continue working with your clients, there really is nothing stopping you from working for yourself at the same time.

And this is why it is important that, over time, you consider shifting your priorities away from providing services and start giving a higher priority to creating products. As a freelancer, your hourly rate will start to top out at some point and selling products—digital or physical—may be one of the best ways for you to continue growing your income moving forward.

Each of these individual products may only provide a trickle of passive income, but the idea is that they can continue to generate an income with no further work needed on your part. In the context of a freelance writer, a natural fit would be to write a book or an e-book. Once you go through the process of writing, editing, formatting and publishing the book, you can continue to earn money from that book as long as it is available for purchase through some sort of online or offline marketplace. You could sell books through Lulu, e-books through Kindle, and so on.

But it can go far beyond that, especially for all you creative freelancers out there.

Let's say, for example, that you are a freelance cartoonist or graphic designer. You may already have a blog where you feature some of your work and you get commissioned for custom work all the time from your clients. However, you may also have some great designs of your own that have only existed in digital form on the Internet.

There are many services out there that can take these designs and turn them into physical products. Indeed, there are several print-on-demand type services that don't require you to keep a physical inventory, minimizing your risk when it comes to the products you want to sell. Zazzle.com is a good example of that, giving you the ability to print t-shirts, mugs, buttons and so on. As an artist, you get your own "online store" on Zazzle too.

I'm not saying that you should necessarily stop working with your clients on the work that they would like to get done. That is the very nature of freelancing and it is through this work that you can grow, learn and broaden your horizons. Working with your clients can be richly rewarding for all parties involved, but working on your own personal projects, shifting from services to products, can help to provide you with a steady flow of passive income that can sustain you through the slower times for your business.

Conclusion

The life of a freelance writer isn't an easy one, nor should it be. When I chose to embark on this career, I did not expect everything to always go my way. I recognized that I would have to endure the slings and arrows of outrageous fortune and I fully understood that even though this is a home-based business where I largely set my own working hours, it is *still a business.*

That means that the income can be inconsistent. That means that I have to wear many hats beyond that of the writer, including the marketer, the administrator, the accountant and social media manager. But it's all worth it.

As you set off on your own freelance journey, you will encounter your own share of challenges and frustrations. The road can be bumpy, but now you have been provided with a basic travel guide that can help you navigate through these points of confusion. Through this guide, you've learned how to prepare a proper working space, how to value your work, how to establish yourself as an expert, how to provide rate quotes, how to stay motivated and how to earn more money.

This book was never meant to be utterly comprehensive, because that is simply not possible. Ultimately, you will have to discover your own path, but at least you are now prepared to venture beyond the margins and slice out your own stake in the wide (and wild) world of freelancing.

About the Author

Michael Kwan is a professional freelance writer who has been writing quality content on the Internet since 1999. He covers a wide range of subject matter, including social commentary, consumer electronics, social media, home-based business, Internet marketing, and consumer advice. He likes to call himself a professional gadget geek.

His work has been published on such prominent websites as Mobile Magazine, MEGATechNews, LoveToKnow, Smartlife Blog, Blogging Tips, Sitepoint, Hadouken Online and John Chow dot Com. You may have seen Michael featured on media outlets like CBC Vancouver, The Commentary and Miss 604.

Michael resides in the Vancouver area in British Columbia, Canada.

Official Website:
http://michaelkwan.com

Official Blog:
http://btr.michaelkwan.com

Social Media:
http://twitter.com/michaelkwan
http://facebook.com/mkfreelance
http://youtube.com/nte604
http://flickr.com/beyondtherhetoric
http://pinterest.com/mkwan
http://michaelkwan.com/linkedin
http://instagram.com/beyondtherhetoric

Acknowledgements

This book has been a monumental labour of love for me, but there's no way I would have been able to complete it on my own. No man is an island, as they say.

First and foremost, I'd like to thank my loving wife Susanne for her ongoing patience and support. You're always there when I need to bounce ideas or I just need a reassuring hug. Thank you.

I'd also like to thank Lesley and Dylan. You don't know one another, but the two of you help to maintain my sanity through our online conversations. Your respective input during the editing process was equally invaluable.

And I'd like to thank you, the reader, for buying this book and reading it clear through to the end. I wish you great success in all your future freelance endeavours.